THE *Judy* & THE *Joy* OF OLIVE OIL & PASTA

THE *Judy* & THE *Joy* OF OLIVE OIL & PASTA

TwiceBakedTwins.com

BY JUDY VIG AND JOY PAOLETTI

Part of *The Judy and The Joy of...* Kitchen Table Book Series
CREATED BY MINDY DICROSTA

Made possible by Old World Olive Co.

THE JUDY AND THE JOY OF PASTA IS PUBLISHED BY TBT/CCN.

COVER PHOTOGRAPH BY JAMIE ARABOLOS

FAMILY PHOTOGRAPHS COURTESY JUDY VIG & JOY PAOLETTI

PHOTOGRAPHS BY JOSEPH LAMBERT IMAGES

PHOTOGRAPH ON PGS: X-1 BY VEER

PHOTOGRAPHS ON PGS: 2-3, 4-5, 23, 25, 26-27 AND 35 BY I-STOCK

DESIGNED BY KIRSTEN NAVIN

ISBN – 978-0-9910402-0-9

PRINTED IN THE UNITED STATES.

Our wonderful
and loving family

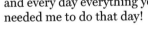

The Judy

Thank you to my children

NICK: For your endless amount of patience and praise

JIMMY: For listening each and every time you called about my recipes when all you really wanted to know, "what's for dinner"

DANIELLE: Please stop asking me, "Mom did you sell any books yet? and when can we go shopping?"

The Joy

Thank you to my children

PAULETTE: Thank you for offering to help with anything we asked!

CRISTYN: For printing the book text over and over again even though you kept saying, "Mom, just read it on the computer!"

PAIGE: For all the creative word suggestions you helped with when my old tired brain couldn't think anymore!

CAYLA: For being patient when I forgot each and every day everything you needed me to do that day!

And to our Mom, the best Mom in the whole world, for endless phone calls explaining the family memories behind the recipes.

We are the Twice Baked Twins, Judy Vig and Joy Paoletti, identical twins with a passion for food and cooking. Growing up in an Italian household, our family time was centered around the dinner table. Dad went to work while mom stayed home; so dinner time became the best part of the day, because that was when we were all together.

Mom cooked every night (move over June Cleaver!) and insisted on a well-balanced meal: which meant a protein, two vegetables and a starch were routinely on our plates. Something delicious was always on the stove bubbling away in the biggest pot. We would talk about what happened that day, cheerleading and what we were planning to wear the next day to school. Poor dad, how bored he must have been! Dad had five sisters so he was truly out numbered from birth; but what a life it was, full of food, fun and family.

We are busy moms, just like most of you, and have been juggling family, home and our work as television lifestyle chefs and food writers for many years. Don't be fooled by the fact that you can't tell us apart, we are identical twins but with completely opposite approaches to just about everything we do. *The Judy and the Joy of...Kitchen Table Series* will bring you two perspectives to classic dishes.

THE JUDY: The shortcut, designed to help you to accomplish anything when time is at a minimum. *I take you from A-to-Z, in and out of the kitchen—fast, but without sacrificing presentation. "I don't want it fine, I want it fabulous!"*

THE JOY: The traditional way, for when you are able to plan ahead and let it simmer all day long. *I take you on a journey back in time to my grandmother's kitchen. Perfect for when there is plenty of time, money is no object, and the sky's the limit. For those with a love of detail, dedication and craftsmanship—this is the approach for you.*

We are proud to be partnered with the The Pink Fund Breast Cancer Association. Judy is a breast cancer survivor (thankfully). Our journey as survivor and caregiver inspired us to share our family recipes and our experiences (including the importance of laughter and inner well-being), with other women facing similar challenges. You will find versions of our recipes that follow healthy guidelines and offer suggestions for people in need of changing their eating habits. We do not claim to be medical experts, nor nutritionists, only passionate solution seekers and creators of recipes and products designed to make life after diagnosis easier. We know firsthand the effects, and affects, breast cancer has on the people touched by this disease.

A NOTE FROM JUDY:

"Joy thinks her traditional way of life is best, and frankly, I don't. I prefer to take the shortest, and quickest way possible and I'm always right."

A NOTE FROM JOY:

"Judy is wrong!"

It is with the long-time support and guidance of our parents and grandparents that we have pursued our love of cooking. With one sister, and seven children between us, we have cooked, baked, ached and faced every imaginable hurdle when it comes to: dinners, parties, lunches, brunches, and everything from sweet 16s to elegant bridal showers. Now in *The Judy and the Joy of...Kitchen Table Book Series*, we give it to you straight—just in two different ways. Try them both and see which suits your personal style, perhaps even a combination of both.

We "Twin"cerely wish you The Judy and The Joy of life!

My partner and I have worked with Judy and Joy, The Twice Baked Twins, for many years. Helping them achieve their goal of sharing their spirit, spunk and succulent recipes with busy moms and businesswomen is a partnership of which we are very proud.

*The Judy and the Joy of...*Kitchen Table Book Series was created to showcase the twin's culinary talents, both the long and short(cut) of it. O.K. truth be told, while these two amazing women have shared their cooking methods and madness with their television and newspaper fans, getting them to write a book series (because a regular cookbook just wouldn't be enough for this dynamic duo) became my challenge. And since Judy, Joy and I share the same birthday, I became the third twin and joined them on this incredible journey!

Judy and Joy have done it all, and are a true life-line for anyone in need of help with time-saving tips and tricks in-and-out of the kitchen. Judy and Joy are both breast cancer survivors. Judy as the one actually afflicted with the disease, and Joy as her loving caretaker, supporter and biggest cheerleader. The road from diagnosis to cancer-free was not always an easy one, but with a double dose of love, laughter and grace they made it—together.

This series is special in its approach because sharing their great recipes is just the beginning. Helping others in similar situations, by sharing their wit, wisdom and of course their food, was the genesis of this book. Giving back then became an integral part of the series. The Twice Baked Twins and our company, Creative Connections Network, are honored to help support The Pink Fund in their mission to provide short-term financial aid to breast cancer patients in active treatment.

The first title of the kitchen table book series, *The Judy and the Joy of Olive Oil & Pasta*, has been made possible by the generous support of Old World Olive Co., illustrating that when motivated people come together, in time, we can move mountains.

Mindy DiCrosta and Les Carter

SUPPORTED BY

OLD WORLD OLIVE CO.

TO BENEFIT

the PINK FUND

REAL HELP NOW

hile traveling the world some years back, we realized that the flavors of the Tuscan Region were so near and dear to our hearts we had to find a way to bring them home with us. Thus Old World Olive Press, now Old World Olive Co. was born.

Upon meeting Judy and Joy we knew instantly that we were kindred spirits. Their love of food and all things flavorful was so in line with why we started Old World Olive Co. (OWOC). Making food fun again is easy when you have the right tools, ingredients and attitude.

When they invited us to work with them on a pasta recipe book we knew it was the perfect partnership to showcase the highest quality, pure extra virgin olive oils and balsamic vinegars that OWOC is known for. The twin's banter, wit and renowned expertise in Italian cuisine, combined with our over 50 flavors of oils and vinegars came together easily in their already tasty dishes.

Each of the recipes in this cookbook features an olive oil, balsamic vinegar or both. We hope you begin to enjoy not only the robust and varied flavors we provide, but realize the health benefits that are an added benefit to good taste.

Shasta and Cory

ld World Olive Co. works with partners in both hemispheres to bring you the freshest, most flavorful, and healthy array of olive oils and balsamic vinegars from around the world. Regional extra virgin olive oils may vary from season to season, but you can always count on us to bring you the freshest oils available.

REGIONAL EXTRA VIRGIN OLIVE OILS:

Arbeqina • Manzanillo • Hojiblanca
Picual • Cortina • Koroneiki
Frantoio • Pacholine • Arbosona
Nocellara del Belice

FLAVORED/SPECIALTY OLIVE OILS

Herbs de Provence • Persian Lime • Basil
Wild Mushroom and Sage • Blood Orange
Meyer Lemon • Roasted Walnut • Chipotle
Tuscan Herb • Cilantro & Roasted Onion
Tunisian Harissa • Garlic • White Truffle
Natural Butter Flavor • Porcini Mushroom
Roasted Sesame • Grapeseed

BALSAMIC VINEGARS

Raspberry • 18 Year Traditional
Cinnamon Pear • Dark Chocolate • Jalapeno
Pomegranate • Golden Pineapple • Fig
Lavender • Black Currant
Honey Ginger White • Summer Peach
Wild Blueberry • Sicilian Lemon • Coconut
Vanilla Bean • Strawberry • Red Apple
Cranberry Pear • Tangerine
Asian Blackberry • Oregano • Espresso
Mango • Serrano Honey • Cara Cara
Orange Vanilla

Thank you for touring our store!

THE SKINNY ON OLD WORLD OLIVE CO.

O ur products are uniquely popular, and of the finest quality. We fondly refer to our store as a food connoisseur's playground. However, we are not just for serious chefs, we want to help the everyday cook discover their inner "foodie", and experience the great flavors, great variety, and a little of the authenticity from the old world olive country.

Our goal is to not only provide a great product and service, but to also help our customers learn how to easily use them in their everyday lives. The simple substitutions we've suggested can make huge health difference in your life.

With over 50 authentic flavors of pure extra virgin olive oils and premium balsamic vinegars showcased in each of our stores' tasting rooms; you'll soon discover there is a flavor for every palette.

"We believe our customers are not only health conscious, but they want a better food experience. Our goal is to continually provide only the highest quality, healthiest products. And we are dedicated to ensure that only the freshest oils and balsamic vinegars are represented in our stores." In order to do this Shasta and Cory work with artisan farms from around the world–who harvest only at the peak of harvest in a first press, cold press, old world procedure.

So come in and experience for yourself the flavors of the world, and the vast opportunities for you to rediscover your love of all things food again. Authentic old world awaits your visit at Old World Olive Co. Five locations in Michigan to better serve you, or visit us at www.oldworldoliveco.com.

DOWNTOWN MARKET
435 Ionia NW
Grand Rapids MI 49503
616-214-8403

GRAND RAPIDS
108 Monroe Center
Grand Rapids MI 49503
616-551-2648

BIRMINGHAM
282 W Maple
Birmingham MI 48012
248-792-2192

ROCKFORD
65 E Bridge Street
Rockford MI 49341
616-884-0107

PLYMOUTH
467 Forest Street
Plymouth MI 48009
734-667-2755

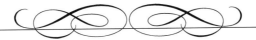

If it were not for the countless people and professionals we have met along the way who have extended: hours of their time, expertise, baking assistance, discounts on services (that were truly above and beyond), innumerable connections that opened doors, friendship, love, advice and a continued belief in us (and what we do), we would not be where we are today. Over the years there has become too many to list, and we wouldn't want to risk leaving anyone out. You know who you are, and please know so do we. We are eternally grateful to all of you.

To our partner, and friend, Mindy DiCrosta, our Mindela, thank you so much for always believing in us. From that first day we stepped into your New York office until today, your patience, guidance and creativity is endless. With all our love, Judy & Joy

Many thanks to Les Carter, Kirsten Navin, Sue Bolen and Marcy Ricardi for all of their love and support...and patience with the two of us!

CONTENTS

OLD WORLD OLIVE CO.

Look for healthy tips and inventive substitutions
from Old World Olive Co. throughout this book.

CONTENTS

RASPBERRY

This thick, rich, perfectly balanced Balsamic Vinegar, bursts with the delicate flavor of fresh, ripe raspberries.

Both sweet and tart, its perfect tossed with mixed salad greens and a little feta cheese. Also enjoy paired with one of our flavored oils or as a marinade or glaze for pork or chicken.

Mix with Walnut or Almond oil, Meyer Lemon or Garlic Extra Virgin Olive Oil.

Olive Oil

The Judy and the Joy of Olive Oil and Pasta takes you on a delicious journey. It is always one recipe 2 ways. Each section showcases *The Judy:* a healthy or time saving twist vs. *The Joy:* a simmer, all day traditional take, on the same recipe.

In the Olive Oil section we get creative and have fun with food. What if you could take a few of your favorite baking ingredients and make something that could help keep your skin in tip-top shape? Polish your table or even soothe a sore throat!

Now you can...so don't put those ingredients away!

Brownies

THE JUDY

Has this ever happened to you? You are just about finished mixing a batch of brownies and just when you reach for the vegetable oil: "OMG...there isn't any left, now what? Can I use olive oil?" Yes you can! Adding olive oil to your brownies in place of vegetable oil will work just fine. A mild light olive oil has a mellow flavor and will make a more dense, fudgy brownie. It is delicious, and I love that I can make a small, but healthy change to this old time classic.

OLIVE OIL & COCOA BROWNIES

3	large eggs		1½	cups unbleached flour
1½	cups sugar		½	cup cocoa powder
½	cup extra virgin olive oil		1	teaspoon kosher salt
2	teaspoons pure vanilla extract		½	cup cacao nibs (optional)

Pre-heat oven to 350°F. Coat an 8-inch square baking dish with olive oil. Cut a piece of parchment to fit just the bottom of the dish and oil that too.

Beat the eggs in a heavy duty mixer for a minute. Increase speed to medium-high while adding the sugar ½ cup at a time. Beat until the eggs are pale, thick and creamy. Decrease mixer speed and slowly add the oil in a thin stream, as if you were making an emulsion-like mayonnaise. Add the vanilla extract.

Sift together the flour, cocoa and salt into a bowl. Stir into the egg mixture until incorporated, scraping down the bowl as needed. Pour the batter into the prepared baking dish and sprinkle with the cacao nibs over the top (if using).

Bake: 25-30 minutes, or until a toothpick inserted into the center of the brownies emerges with some moist crumbs. Cool the pan completely on a rack before cutting into serving pieces

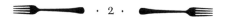

Add your favorite nuts for crunch and a protein boost!!

Judy's Tips & Tricks

Brownies

THE JOY

There is nothing better than a warm brownie enjoyed by a roaring fire in the winter, or with a dollop of creamy, cold ice cream in the summer. Brownies are so versatile and a "go to" recipe for many. You can add almost anything to the batter: nuts, chips, even chopped cookies and pretzels. Frost and sprinkle with any thing you like! You can even change the shape for a more creative presentation and a smidge more elegant!

MY FAVORITE BROWNIE RECIPE

½	cup butter or margarine		1	teaspoon vanilla extract
⅓	cup premium cocoa		½	cup all-purpose flour
1	cup granulated sugar		1/4	teaspoon salt
2	eggs		1/2	cup nuts, chopped

Preheat oven to 350°F. Grease one 8-inch square baking pan.

In a medium saucepan melt the butter over low heat (or melt in microwave in a one-quart container).

Remove the melted butter from heat, add the cocoa, and stir until well-blended. Add the sugar and mix well. Add the eggs, one at a time, beating well after each addition. Stir in the vanilla, flour and salt. DO NOT OVERBEAT. Fold in the nuts.

Spread in prepared pan and bake: 25-30 minutes, or until wooden toothpick tests done.

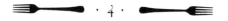

OLD WORLD OLIVE CO.

Go Gourmet!

Add additional flavor to your brownies by substituting our Blood Orange EVOO or even our Tunisian Harissa olive oil for a spicy chocolate brownie—the perfect combination of sweet and savory.

On the second day, cut a piece and hide in a napkin in your hand. Take a bite and wave to kids as the school bus pulls away!

Joy's Tips & Tricks

· 5 ·

Coffee Cake

THE JUDY

There are several reasons I love substituting olive oil for butter, or shortening, when I bake. First, it is always the correct temperature. Most recipes call for room temperature butter, and who has room temperature butter readily available? Second, by cutting the saturated fat and cholesterol, I feel less guilty about eating a piece (or two)!

This cake has a moist texture, and a sweet, yet pleasingly, tart bite from the lemon. Most of my days begin with this delicious cake along with my morning cuppa. I hope yours will too!

OLIVE OIL CAKE COFFEE CAKE

1 cup all purpose flour	½ cup extra virgin olive oil (I used 1/4 cup lemon oil & 1/4 cup orange oil)
½ cup almond flour	½ cup lemon juice
1 cup vanilla sugar	Zest of 1 lemon
½ teaspoon salt	2 eggs
1 teaspoon baking soda	Powdered sugar for garnish
1 teaspoon baking powder	
2 teaspoons vanilla extract	

Pre-heat the oven to 350°F. Oil a 9-inch cake pan and line the bottom with parchment paper.

In a large bowl, combine the dry ingredients and stir until combined. Make a well in the dry ingredients and add in the wet ingredients. Beat on medium low until everything is combined. Do not over beat.

Pour the cake batter into the oiled pan. Place in the oven and bake: 45 minutes.

The cake is done once the edges have browned and pull slightly away from the sides of the pan. If testing with a toothpick, it should come out clean. Let the cake sit for a few minutes, then run a thin knife around the sides of the cake to loosen. Carefully remove the cake from pan, place on serving dish and sprinkle with powdered sugar.

For a special presentation, use a bundt pan—just make sure to oil extremely well.

 It will take a few less minutes in the oven too if you use a bundt pan! A quicker coffee cake for when you just can't wait!

DID YOU KNOW?

Most coffee cake recipes do not contain coffee as an ingredient? The very first coffee cakes were made with honey, boiled raisins, dates and nuts—making them more like the fruit cake we know today. It was baked in a single layer pan, usually square or rectangle.

Serve the cake warm (my preference), or allow it to cool then serve

Judy's Tips & Tricks

Coffee Cake

THE JOY

Dessert is a big deal in our family. Before every holiday, Mom calls a meeting to plan the food. She sits at the head of the table with her paper and pen (yes, I said paper and pen, she wants nothing to do with computers) and the first item on the agenda is to plan the desserts. Her coffee cake is always on the list (justifiably so, as it is the most requested item). She uses her grandmother's recipe which has been in our family for generations. We love listening to her describe our great-grandmother Nellie, beating the cake by hand with her big strong arms. This was the secret behind why her cake would always rise so high! Everyone who has tried this cake love it. Mom always said, "a batter that is delicious raw,* will be even more amazing when baked". Well, this cake is scrumptious, so put on a big pot of coffee and enjoy!

OLD FASHIONED SOUR CREAM COFFEE CAKE

2	cups all-purpose flour		1/2	cup butter
1	teaspoon baking powder		2	large eggs
1	teaspoon baking soda		2	teaspoons vanilla extract
1/4	teaspoon salt		1	cup sour cream
1 1/2	cups sugar			

In a medium size bowl, mix together the flour, baking powder, baking soda and salt, set aside.

In a large bowl, cream the butter and sugar. Add the eggs, one at a time, and beat after each. Add the vanilla and sour cream, mix. Add the dry ingredients and mix until combined.

Make topping (see below).

Pour cake batter into prepared pan and sprinkle with topping. Or add half of the batter, sprinkle with topping, pour rest of batter on top, sprinkle with remaining topping and bake.

One 12-cup tube pan, buttered and floured

Set a rack in the middle of the oven and preheat to 350°F. Bake for 50-60 minutes.

TOPPING

1	cup (about 4-5 ounces) roasted walnuts, coarsely chopped
1/4	cup brown sugar
2	teaspoons ground cinnamon

Sprinkle the walnuts onto a cookie sheet and bake in the oven for about 10 minutes. Watch carefully, they can brown fast. Let cool then mix with the sugar and cinnamon

* *Do not eat raw batter, it may contain salmonella bacteria*

DID YOU KNOW?

Coffee cake was offered as a gesture of kindness to family and friends. The cake would be served at the coffee table, or on an elaborately dressed table, set with fine china. No matter how coffee cake is served, it remains one of the world's most popular, and delicious, cakes ever.

OLD WORLD OLIVE CO.

HEALTHY TIPS AND SUBSTITUTIONS

Add a couple tablespoons of balsamic vinegar to the nuts
when roasting to add flavor and an irresistible sweetness.
For this recipe, try Espresso or Cinnamon Pear.

Butter EVOO + balsamic vinegar = reduced bad fats and sugar.

Roasting the
walnuts before you
use them really
brings out
the flavor.

Joy's Tips & Tricks

· 9 ·

Chocolate Chip Cookies

THE JUDY

After you read my recipe I know you will be saying to yourself, "Really? These cookies taste good?" They are totally my choice over the traditional! The olive oil adds a great depth of flavor and creates a chewy, yet crunchy texture. I just can't describe it, so I won't. Just make a batch and try them for yourself. They taste great, and more importantly, I don't feel guilty about eating the whole batch!

OLIVE OIL CHOCOLATE CHIP COOKIES

2	cup all-purpose flour		³/₄	cup vanilla sugar*
1	teaspoons salt		³/₄	cup brown sugar
1	teaspoon baking soda		2	eggs
¹/₄	cup extra virgin olive oil (recommended blood orange or butter EVOO		1 or 2	tablespoons of vanilla almond milk
1	tablespoon vanilla extract		1	cup chocolate chips

Preheat the oven to 375°F.

Combine the flour, baking soda, and salt in a medium bowl and set aside.

Combine the sugars, vanilla, and olive oil and beat mixture at medium speed: 2 minutes. Beat in eggs one a time. Gradually beat in the flour mixture, then add a tablespoon of milk. If the dough is a little dry, add a bit more milk(I used 1 tablespoon + 1 teaspoon). Stir in the chips.

Roll cookie dough into balls and place on a greased or lined baking sheet and bake:10-12 minutes, until lightly golden.

DID YOU KNOW?

The chocolate chip cookie has been a favorite for decades. Some people add oatmeal, M&M's, nuts & raisins and even peanut butter to their recipe. Anything added tastes good.... how could it not?

OLD WORLD OLIVE CO.

Take your cookies to the Tropics!
Try using Persian Lime EVOO and white chocolate chips and indulge in a tangy, sweet treat. Your taste buds will think you're on vacation.

DID YOU KNOW?

The traditional cookie was invented (accidentally) in 1934 by Ruth Wakefield, who owned the Toll House Inn in Whitman, Massachusetts. Ruth Wakefield ran out of her baking chocolate and replaced it with a chocolate bar that was given to her by Andrew Nestle. Hmmmmm........ that name sounds familiar, doesn't it? She served the cookies to her guests and they became an instant success.

During World War II, GIs from Massachusetts shared these cookies with soldiers from other parts of the United States. Soon hundreds of GI's were writing home about the crunchy little cookie asking for more. And the nation-wide craze began.

Chocolate Chip Cookies

THE JOY

The chocolate chip cookie is definitely the all-American cookie. We see it everywhere: at every family parties, picnics, and on holiday dessert tables (it definitely makes an appearance on my sweets platter). This recipe was given to me by my friend Cheryl, almost 30 years ago; I have experimented with the recipe over the years to get it just the way my family likes it! I think I have finally found the right texture and sweetness. I know this will become a favorite of your family's too. Enjoy!

JOY'S FAVORITE CHOCOLATE CHIP COOKIES

2 cups flour	1 teaspoon baking soda
1 bar butter flavored Crisco (1 cup)	2-3 teaspoons vanilla extract
2 cups vanilla sugar*	12 ounces good quality chocolate, chopped
1 egg	1 cup nuts, any kind, optional
1 teaspoon salt	

Preheat oven to 350°F and line a cookie sheet with parchment paper.

Beat Crisco and sugar until fluffy: 3 minutes. Add the egg and vanilla extract, mix until combined.

In a separate bowl combine the dry ingredients, blend thoroughly and add to the mixer. Stir just until incorporated. Add the chunks of chocolate, and nuts (if using), mix with a spoon until combined.

Roll into a 1½ inch ball onto the prepared cookie sheet and bake: 19-20 minutes or until golden (oven temperatures vary). So stay close by and watch them.

So delicious when dunked into ice cold milk!

When baking any treat, it always comes out best when all the ingredients are room temperature.

Joy's Tips & Tricks

DO NOT OVER MIX.

Over mixing will lend to a tough batter.

Apple Crumble

DID YOU KNOW?

An apple crumble is fruit on the bottom and an oat streusel crumbled on top; or is that a cobbler? or is it maybe a crisp? Do you know the difference? First let's start with the what these desserts have in common—the fruit is always on the bottom and they are baked in a baking dish. Now to their differences. Crisps and crumbles both have streusel topping, however a crumble also has oats. A cobbler on the other hand, uses biscuit dropped on top of the fruit to form a crust that looks like cobble stones!

THE JUDY

Apple anything is one of my favorite choices for dessert. I love my Mother's apple pie, and my grandmother's apple cake is to die for. First she dips the apple slices in a sugar and cinnamon mixture, and then places them on top of the batter. I remember her making this all the time when I was a child. As much as I love these recipes the way they are, I wanted to cut down on the fat and sugar to make it a healthier option for me (so I can have it more often). So here it is...baked apple with a crumble topping. For the crumble, I used almond flour, no sugar and a heart-healthy olive oil plus a few other ingredients to spice it up. This one is totally delish and so healthy too.

BAKED APPLES WITH AN OLIVE OIL CRUMBLE TOPPING

4 large apples, cored and hollowed out	$^1/_2$ teaspoon apple pie spice
$^2/_3$ cup flour (I used regular white)	1 teaspoon vanilla extract
$^2/_3$ cup almond meal	$^1/_2$ teaspoon orange extract
$^2/_3$ cup oats	$^1/_2$ cup olive oil
$^1/_4$ teaspoon salt	

Place all of the ingredients, except the oil(!), in the food processor and give it a whirl. Add the olive oil in a slow drizzle until the mixture clumps....now STOP! It's done. Stuff the apples.

Preheat oven to 375°F. Coat the bottom of baking dish with olive oil, and place stuffed apples in dish. Add $^1/_4$ cup water to bottom of baking pan. Bake for about 40 minutes. Spoon juices over top before serving.

P.S. I added a handful of nuts for added crunch!

Baked apples
are great served
as a side dish
with pork or
turkey.

Judy's Tips & Tricks

OLD WORLD OLIVE CO.

Use Herbs De Provence EVOO to make it just the right
amount of savory—no garlic—so it's not overpowering. The herbal notes
heighten the natural flavor of the apples. If using this, omit apple pie
spice and vanilla, instead add a pinch of nutmeg. Drizzle with Apple
Balsamic for a finishing touch. It's like fall on a plate.

Apple Crumble

THE JOY

I have been baking this dessert for family and friends for a number of years now, always adding a bit more of this, or a pinch more of that. I think I finally got it just right! Somehow though, over the years, my younger sister Jackie took over baking this dish. It was our Dad's favorite, and sadly, since he passed away, Jackie stopped making it. She just couldn't...she tried once, but cried through the whole process. This year, after Judy survived her breast cancer, she can't seem to get enough apple anything. Soooooo...my baby sister will be making this recipe again for Judy. Now, if there are any tears, they will be tears of Joy and gratitude. Yayyyyy!

DADDY'S FAVORITE APPLE CRUMBLE

2½ pounds apples, your favorite variety, peeled, cored & sliced	½-1 teaspoon grated lemon rind
1 cup vanilla sugar*	a good splash of fresh lemon juice
2 teaspoons apple pie spice	2 tablespoons cornstarch mixed with ¼ cup water

Preheat oven to 350°F. Butter a 9x13-inch decorative baking dish, or any size (the apples will bake down so don't worry).

Place the apples in a large skillet on medium heat, sprinkle with lemon juice.

Combine the sugar, pie spice and lemon rind in a small bowl, sprinkle over the apples and toss to coat. Bring this mixture to a boil, uncovered, about 5 minutes. Add the cornstarch/water mixture and stir to blend. Pour into prepared baking dish. Set aside.

Sprinkle the crubble topping (below) over the apples. Bake: 30 minutes, or until top is golden and the apples are soft.

CRUMBLE TOPPING

¾ cup brown sugar	pinch of salt
¾ cup flour	½-1 teaspoon cinnamon
½ cup melted butter	¾ nuts *(optional)*
½-1 teaspoon vanilla extract	

Melt the butter and let it cool slightly. Add the vanilla extract.

Add butter to dry mixture and blend. Taste it! Add a bit more of whatever flavor you like.

DID YOU KNOW?
The Second World War influenced the creation of the apple crumble? In Britain during WWII, food was rationed, so there just wasn't enough ingredients going around to make an apple pie. Out of necessity, the apple crumble was invented. It took a lot less flour to make, and was less expensive too.

Using a
few different
varieties of apples
gives a wonderful
melody of flavors
and textures.

Joy's Tips & Tricks

Body Scrub

THE JUDY

I totally love this body scrub because everything in it is good for you, plus it's safe enough to eat . Could it get any better? As soon I mixed ingredients together, I was imagining myself enjoying a big delicious slice of my mother's banana bread slathered in butter. But this recipe has no calories; it goes on your body, not in.

The bananas are creamy and blend nicely with the olive oil giving the scrub a nice, luxurious feel. The sugar, sea salt and nuts add the right amount of texture for a great scrub, while the vanilla and cinnamon makes the experience just delicious!

P.S. *I added the salt last so I could eat some of the mixture. Don't tell anyone!*

BANANA NUT BREAD BODY SCRUB

2-3	bananas
1	teaspoon olive oil
³/₄	granulated sugar
¹/₂	cup course sea salt

¹/₈	cup ground walnuts *(optional)*
1	teaspoon of vanilla extract
¹/₂	teaspoon of cinnamon

Mash the bananas with a fork in a bowl. Add the remaining ingredients. Put in an air tight container and store in the fridge for 2-3 days.

Use a plastic container. The scrub may be a little slippery, due to the olive oil, and could slip out of your hands in the bath or shower.

DID YOU KNOW?

Making your own body scrub is easier than you think. It's certainly less expensive than buying one, or going to a spa. But more importantly, it is chemical-free, made only with natural ingredients.

Banana flesh is very hydrating and great for wrinkles as a topical treatment. It improves the texture of skin by toning it up and adds a healthy glow!

Don't throw
the peels away.
Cut a piece off and
hold over a pimple, it
will help reduce the
inflammation.

Judy's Tips & Tricks

OLD WORLD OLIVE CO.

Add a fresh burst of citrus to this scrub by using
Blood Orange or Meyer Lemon EVOO.
The added aroma of citrus creates a refreshing scent.

Banana Bread

THE JOY

These tender little cakes are super moist. The healthy flours and the coconut oil are great choices for baking any sweet treat. Topped with a drizzle of local honey, and garnished with a few periwinkle flowers; the presentation is really the top banana. Plus, they're gluten free!

DID YOU KNOW?

Banana Bread recipes became very popular in the 1960s when hearty breads were all the rage. It has a thick batter and is a cross between a cake and a bread. Every family is proud of their own unique recipe. Our Grandmother's bread was more of a sweet bread, while her sister's was more of a high-rise cake. Whichever recipe your family holds dear, banana bread still brings comfort and a trip back to childhood!

BABY BANANA BUNDT CAKES

2 medium bananas, mashed	1½ teaspoons baking soda
2 tablespoons coconut oil, melted	½ teaspoon salt
1 tablespoon honey	1 teaspoon cinnamon
1 tablespoon vanilla extract	¼ cup chopped almonds *(optional)*
3 eggs	honey for drizzle
1 cup almond flour	edible flowers for garnish
½ cup coconut flour	

Preheat oven to 350°F. Grease mini bundt pans, set aside.

Mix together the bananas, coconut oil, honey, vanilla, and eggs until completely combined. Add the almond flour, coconut flour, baking soda, salt, and cinnamon stir until all the ingredients are fully incorporated.

Spoon the mixture (which should be thick) into the prepared mini bundt pans and smooth the top. Sprinkle the chopped almonds over the top. Fills about five mini bundt pans.

Bake for 20-25 minutes or until the bread is golden brown and a knife comes out clean. Let cool for 10 minutes, then invert onto a wire rack to cool completely.

Drizzle with honey and garnish with edible flowers (*if using*).

OLD WORLD OLIVE CO.

HEALTHY TIPS AND SUBSTITUTIONS

Not a fan of Coconut? Try using our Almond or Walnut Oil

Ripe bananas bring a sweeter flavor to the bread, but if you don't have any on hand, place the unripe fruit in a brown paper bag for a bit.

Joy's Tips & Tricks

DID YOU KNOW?

Olive oil alone can be used as a makeup remover (and it works beautifully), but when mixed with coconut oil, this delightful mash is now fantastic!

Coconut oil is a natural plant based oil and is great for hydration.

Olive oil is full of polyphenols which are an antioxidant, as well as anti-inflamma-tory. In the skin care world even the word inflammation is known to cause wrinkles!

The combination of these two ingredients glide across your skin, and break down the makeup; making it easy to remove when using a tissue or a cotton ball.

Olive Oil and Coconut Smash

THE JUDY

I use a waterproof foundation everyday, and rarely go out without it. One day, I realized I didn't recognize any of the ingredients in my makeup remover. My remover? The one my mom said was perfect for me to use at 13-years old? Oh my gosh, have I really been putting all those chemicals on my face for that long? My Mom needs to re-think this, I certainly have. I love the way this Olive and Coconut Oil Smash makeup remover is so smooth and velvety, it melts deliciously into your skin the second you put it on. I wipe it away with a tissue and cleanse as usual.

OLIVE OIL AND COCONUT SMASH MAKEUP REMOVER

    6   parts coconut oil (6 tablespoons)
    2   parts light olive oil (2 tablespoons)

Place both ingredients in a small bowl. Smash together with a spatula until mixed.

This makes a great gift for a birthday girl. Especially one who just started to use face make-up. I like to store in fun shaped plastic containers for the teenagers—it could be a little slippery and drop!

For a firmer texture, keep your smash in the refriger- ator, or in the cabinet for a softer mixture.

Judy's Tips & Tricks

Olive Oil Mayonnaise

THE JOY

Store-bought mayo is incredibly nasty. Aside from the questionable ingredients, those mayos are made with industrial oils—completely toxic and awful for your body.

I love this recipe for mayonnaise. The thought of giving up our favorite summer picnic salads was something we just couldn't imagine. Now we don't have to; tuna, macaroni, potato and chicken salads will live on in our homes with this clean, great-tasting mayonnaise.

This recipe uses amazingly-healthy coconut oil and real olive oil, along with fresh pastured eggs. A pastured egg is from a chicken that is allowed to roam in an open field, the way you might imagine a chicken would want to live!

A HEALTHY MAYONNAISE? YES!

1 whole, pastured egg
2 pastured egg yolks
1 tablespoon Dijon mustard
Juice of 1/2 small lemon
1/2 teaspoon sea salt

Pepper to taste
1/2 cup quality olive oil
1/2 cup coconut oil, extra-virgin or refined
Secret ingredient:
1 tablespoon plain whole milk yogurt

Melt your coconut oil over a very low heat setting, just so it turns from a solid to a liquid. Do not let it get hot, or it will cook the eggs. Slowly pour the oils into your food processor/blender while is running at low speed. It is important this is done very slowly; just pouring a very thin stream. Once the oils are emulsified, add the yogurt. Yogurt gives the mayonnaise a semi-sweet and tangy flavor and helps it to stay fresh.

Pastured eggs
are available at
Whole Foods, and
other specality
grocery stores.

Joy's Tips & Tricks

Body Butter

DID YOU KNOW?

Our skin is the largest organ in our body. it protects everything inside of us. We need to take care of it properly, so it will continue to take care of us. Unfortunately, many body lotions contain toxic chemicals full of carcinogens. Read the ingredients on the back of the bottle—you won't recognize any.

This is what led us to create our own body lotion; so people would know exactly what is going on their skin, and what was being absorbed into their body.

THE JUDY

Have you ever really looked at all the lotions you have in your bathroom? I must have ten! One for my body, one for my hands, one specifically for my feet, the list goes on and on. Like most of you, I have been slathering this stuff on for years. Really? This is ridiculous and I headed straight to my kitchen to test out some homemade recipes. I had most of the ingredients right in my home and the rest I ordered online. Within a few days, I was whipping up batches of body butter to die for, and so can you, here's how.

WHIPPED CHOCOLATE BODY BUTTER

1	cup cocoa butter	
1/2	cup coconut oil	
1/2	cup mild/light olive oil	
1	teaspoon of chocolate extract	

Using a double boiler, melt the cocoa butter and the coconut oil until it becomes liquid. Stir in the olive oil.

Chill this in the fridge, just until it begins to harden, but not completely hard. Using any mixer (hand held or standing) mix till peaks form.

Fill any container you like, and chill for an hour or so.

This makes a great gift!

If your house
is warm, keep in the
refrigerator; or it may go
back to a liquid form. If so,
no worries, just chill again
and re-whip!

Judy's Tips & Tricks

· 27 ·

Vanilla Cupcakes

THE JOY

You say, olive oil in a cupcake?" yes! People often want to substitute vegetable oil in their baking recipes with olive oil because they know that olive oil is a 'healthy' oil. It's true that olive oil is a poly-unsaturated fat, which makes it a healthy oil. Olive oil will react in the same way with most baking recipes in the same way as other vegetable oils.

OLIVE OIL VANILLA CUPCAKES

- 2 cups all purpose flour (or substitute gluten-free flour)
- 1 cup vanilla sugar*
- 1 teaspoon baking soda
- 1 teaspoon baking powder
- ½ teaspoon salt

- 2 eggs (or egg substitute)
- 1 cup vanilla soy milk (or any type of milk: dairy, almond, coconut)
- 1 tablespoon vanilla extract
- 3 tablespoons olive oil
- ¼ teaspoon lemon juice

Pre heat oven to 350°F.

Whisk together dry ingredients in a mixing bowl. Add in the wet ingredients (starting with eggs), and beat with a hand mixer until smooth: 2 minutes.

Divide batter evenly into 12-lined muffin cups. Bake: 22-25 minutes, or until tops are lightly browned and a toothpick inserted into the center of the cupcakes comes out clean.

*Vanilla Sugar: 2 cups white sugar, 1-2 fresh vanilla beans, split in half.

VANILLA WHIPPED CREAM FROSTING

- 1 cup heavy cream
- 2 tablespoons agave

- ½ tablespoon coconut extract
- 1 tablespoon vanilla extract

Place the cream, agave and extracts in a large bowl. Whip with a mixer until stiff peaks form. Makes about 2 cups

OLD WORLD OLIVE CO.

HEALTHY TIPS AND SUBSTITUTIONS

Does your recipe call for butter? Substitute with EVOO by using ¼ less than what it calls for. If, for example, the recipe says 1 cup butter, use ¾ cup EVOO. A simple, healthy substitution.

A stiff peak is when you lift the beaters. The peaks should stand straight up.

Joy's Tips & Tricks

Orange Dreamcicle

THE JUDY

Our father had a beautiful voice and loved to sing. He sounded a lot like the Chairman of the Board, Mr. Frank Sinatra. When he was young, he sang at all the ballrooms and night clubs in town, loving every minute of it. His mother, our Gramma, would tell us this about how he would come home with such a sore throat from singing to all the girls!! She would give him a teaspoon of olive oil and tell him to let it to trickle down the back of his throat. I can still see her smiling face as she said, "He always gave me a big kiss and said thanks Ma!"

My youngest son seems to have inherited "the voice" and often asks me for the old-fashioned family remedy. However, I've added a few delicious ingredients so he would like it better. I think you will too!

ORANGE DREAMSICLE SORE THROAT SOOTHER

- 1 tablespoon of olive oil
- ½ teaspoon of honey or agave
- ¼ teaspoon of orange extract
- ¼ teaspoon vanilla extract

Place all of the ingredients in a small cup, mix well. A teaspoon every once in a while does the trick!

DID YOU KNOW?
Olive oil is great for coating and soothing a sore throat that feels dry and scratchy. Just a bit is all you need for some quick relief.

OLD WORLD OLIVE CO.

HEALTHY TIPS AND SUBSTITUTIONS

Can't find orange extract? Simply replace with our Blood Orange EVOO. Our citrus olive oils are made by a process called "fusion". This means the olives are pressed directly with the oranges themselves so essentially it is EVOO and all-natural orange extract in one!

Citrus Dressing

I love all these wonderful, but unusual, flavors for a salad. Orange and vanilla work so great together and adding honey makes it a great combination. Most people do not think of sweet when they think of salad dressings; but I like to think out of the box sometimes and shake up my traditional recipes. The scent of the citrus reminds me of summertime, warm weather and a salad my Nana would make during trips to our family cottage. I have added a few more ingredients to her original recipe and love to serve it anytime of the year.

ARUGULA, FENNEL AND ORANGES WITH A CITRUS DRIZZLE

1 large fennel bulb	4 cups fresh arugula
3 navel oranges	vinaigrette *(see below)*

Cut off the stems and feathery fronds and remove any bruised or discolored outer layers. Cut the fennel bulb in half lengthwise, removing the tough parts of the core. Next cut the bulb in half crosswise, and then into slices about a half inch thick, finally cut the slices into 1-inch pieces.

Peel the oranges and separate sections.

Place the fennel and arugula in a large serving bowl. When ready to serve, drizzle the vinaigrette over the arugula and fennel and toss gently to coat. Arrange the orange slices on top. Drizzle with as much of the remaining vinaigrette as you like and serve right away.

CITRUS VINAIGRETTE

2 teaspoons grated orange zest	1/2 teaspoon vanilla extract
1/4 cup fresh orange or tangerine or clementine juice	2 teaspoons Dijon mustard
2 tablespoons fresh lemon juice	1 shallot, finely chopped
4 tablespoons extra-virgin olive oil	1/2 teaspoon dried tarragon (optional)
	Salt and freshly ground pepper

In a small bowl, whisk together the orange zest, orange juice, lemon juice, olive oil, vanilla, mustard, shallot, and tarragon (if using). Season to taste with salt and pepper. Set aside.

I love to add sliced red pears and sprinkle with nuts at holiday time.

OLD WORLD OLIVE CO.

Try Milanese Gremolata EVOO for an interesting flair.
The hint of mint, lemon, and a little bit of
garlic pairs beautifully with the tarragon.

Joy's Tips & Tricks

Peppermint

THE JUDY

When preparing for our TV cooking segments, Joy and I are on our feet constantly for three days prior to the show. One day is spent shopping for the set: getting dishes, pots, pans, and etc. One day to bring everything back, because Joy changed her mind overnight. And one day to actually bake and test the recipes. Finally, it's show day—and we wear heels! Our feet are tired, hot, sweaty, and they ache...ugh!

During all this, it helps to treat your feet with a soothing rub! I massage a few drops of this on my feet at night before bed. It feels wonderful, enjoy!

PEPPERMINT OIL FOOT RUB

15   drops of peppermint essential oil
     just slightly under 1 ounce of olive oil

Fill a one ounce dropper bottle with olive oil just under full, add peppermint drops. I used 15 peppermint oil drops, add as many as you like. Be careful though, peppermint essential oil is strong. When adding drops, I only add 5 drops add a time then shake the bottle to mix. Take a sniff, add more drops if needed.

After I massage the oil into my feet I put on a pair of nice white cotton socks to keep from ruining my sheets. (I use any color socks that are clean that day!)

This is a great gift for a girlfriend's birthday, add a soft pair of socks to go with it!

Ask your spouse or significant other to do the massage for you…it feels even better!

Judy's Tips & Tricks

Peppermint Gelato

THE JOY

There is something about ice cream, or in this case gelato, that makes everyone smile—including me. Now you know that I love to make everything homemade, and never ever take the easy way out, but just this once I am! Everyone is allowed that once or twice in their lifetime. I happen to like the gelato that is on the market these days. When I go to my favorite store, I buy their best, freshly-made vanilla. Once home, I add peppermint extract and throw in my homemade olive oil chocolate chip cookies and brownies; cut up into chunks.

PEPPERMINT ICE CREAM WITH OLIVE OIL BROWNIES AND COOKIE CHUNKS

- 1 pint vanilla gelato
- 1 teaspoon peppermint
- 1 olive oil chocolate chip cookie, crumbled *(see recipe on page 12)*
- 1 olive oil brownie, crumbled or chopped into small chunks *(see recipe on page 4)*

Soften gelato by leaving out for a bit. Fold in the crumbled cookies, brownie and peppermint. Taste and add more peppermint if you like.

Soften gelato
in microwave for
10 second intervals
until soft.

Joy's Tips & Tricks

Homemade Bug Spray

DID YOU KNOW?

That the United States Army developed the pesticide Deet so they could protect themselves from the jungle in WWII and Vietnam? It is also the go to chemical to create most commercial insect repellents. Deet is a pesticide and a toxic chemical that is absorbed into the skin and then goes right into our blood stream.

THE JOY

After a long day I like to sit out on the back porch, sip my decaf coffee and just listen to all the night air has to offer. Unfortunately, that often means mosquitos here in the north east. As I move into a healthier lifestyle, I know I can make better choices about what I put on my skin. I am going slow. It is very easy to become over whelmed with all these changes, but a homemade mosquito spray oil is definitely one change I am interested in. Making the spray was a lot easier than I thought. It's inexpensive, and I must admit, kind of fun. I loved picking out all of the essential oils used in this potion. Try it, I think you will like it.

HOMEMADE OLIVE OIL BUG SPRAY

4 ounces of distilled water	25 drops clove essential oil
4 ounces Witch Hazel	25 drops cinnamon essential oil
½ teaspoon very light olive oil	

In an 8 oz spray bottle add all ingredients and shake well before each use. I used an olive oil mister

Do not use on children. Wash hands after use.

Always do a
test on yourself for
minor skin irritations.
Do not use on
your face.

Judy's Tips & Tricks

OLD WOR

Simmering Spice Oil

THE JOY

When I want the house to smell like the fall, and feel all warm and cozy; I make my own simmering oil and throw in a few cinnamon sticks and a small handful of cloves. I save all the last few drops (that isn't enough for a recipe) of olive oil from the bottom of the bottle in a little jar. By the time the holidays roll around I have just enough to make spice simmering oil!

It smells wonderful. Go ahead and give it a try!

CINNAMON AND CLOVE SIMMERING OIL

1/2   cup oil
2-3   cinnamon sticks
      small handful of whole cloves

Add all ingredients to your favorite simmer pot and enjoy!

 · 40 ·

OLD WORLD OLIVE CO.

Try our Blood Orange EVOO instead of the orange peel.

Add small pieces of orange peel, star anise ...anything you like!

Joy's Tips & Tricks

$\mathcal{S}$un $\mathcal{P}$rotection

After reading up on some of the ingredients in store bought sunscreens, I decided that I should try to make my own using natural ingredients. I now need to stay out of the sun when it is at its strongest, and enjoy being under an umbrella a bit more; but I find it worth it, knowing I did not slather cancer causing chemicals all over my body.

HOMEMADE SUN PROTECTION

1/2   cup olive oil

1/4   cup beeswax

1/4   cup coconut oil

2   tablespoons of non-nano Zinc Oxide. Do not inhale, I wear a mask.

A few drops of an essential oil. (I like lavender mixed with a bit of vanilla essential oil also!)

Add all ingredients, except the zinc oxide, in a glass jar that is at least a pint or larger. I love the mason jars you can get at the grocery store.

In a medium sauce pan, add a few inches of water and warm over medium heat. Put the glass jar in with the cover on loosely until the ingredients start to melt. Stir a few times to mix. When completely melted add the zinc oxide and stir until combined.

Take out of water carefully, may be hot and let cool. Stir a few times as it is cooling.

Use a mask when working with the Zinc Oxide.

Store in a dry cool space.

I prefer a thicker consistency, so I used a bit more beeswax..

Judy's Tips & Tricks

· 43 ·

Orange Shortbread Cookies

THE JOY

I just love cookies, but a cookie with olive oil? Yes! I try to only make them when I'm having guests over so I don't eat all of them myself. The richness of the olive oil as opposed to butter is great in a shortbread cookie (and I was skeptical at first!). They are wonderfully crunchy with the olive oil and the sea salt is perfectly paired with the sweet cookie. Enjoy!.

ORANGE OLIVE OIL SHORTBREAD COOKIES WITH ITALIAN SEA SALT

3 cups all-purpose flour	1½ teaspoons sea salt
1½ cups confectioners' sugar	2 tablespoons fresh orange juice
1 cup orange olive oil	sanding sugar for garnish

In the bowl of an electric mixer, combine the 1½ cups sugar and olive oil. Beat on low until smooth.

In a separate bowl, combine the flour and sea salt. Gradually add the flour mixture to the olive oil. Beat until combined (it will be crumbly).

Use your hands to roll the dough into a log that is 1-inch in diameter. Roll log in wax paper and refrigerate for one hour.

Preheat oven to 350°. Slice the dough and place on a cookie sheet. Bake for 12 minutes. Remove and place on rack.

Sprinkle with sanding sugar.

I used 1/2 teaspoon orange extract if you do not have orange olive oil.
Judy likes them baked a bit longer, until very golden brown...just saying.

If you can find blood oranges, use them... the taste is even better!

Joy's Tips & Tricks

· 45 ·

Citrus Dressing

THE JUDY

One day, while I was sitting in my kitchen with a freshly perked cup of coffee, reading over my list of chores for the day, I couldn't help but wonder "Why does this coffee taste like furniture polish?" After a second I realized earlier that morning I had polished the table with a can of lemon-scented chemicals. The fumes were killing my perfect cuppa! Time to make a change and make my own polish. It is so easy, and you probably have all the ingredients in your home. Go and take a look in your pantry for some olive oil, white vinegar and lemon. Why not mix up a batch for your furniture and then go use it on your salad for lunch!

OLIVE OIL AND LEMON FURNITURE POLISH

- 1/3 cup distilled white vinegar
- 1/3 cup Olive Oil
- 1 tablespoon fresh lemon juice (no pulp)

Mix in a small spray bottle, shake well before each spray onto a soft cloth and wipe surface.

Store in a cool dry place and make a new batch each month!!

The acidity
in the vinegar and
lemon act as a disinfectant
and deodorizer. Both are
natural cleaners.

Joy's Tips & Tricks

Butter Sauce

THE JOY

Just a drizzle of a wonderfully flavored olive oil can dress up a simple meal and turn it into a great one. Below I used a three cheese ravioli, fried lightly in garlic butter, garnished with Parmesan and fresh parsley. Using a fragrant olive oil drizzle for the finish was just perfect!

THREE CHEESE RAVIOLI IN FRIED BUTTER SAUCE

- 1 pound ravioli, prepared according to package directions
- 2 garlic cloves, minced
- 2-3 tablespoons butter

- parsley, minced for garnish
- Parmesan cheese, garnish
- salt and pepper to taste
- olive oil for drizzle

Prepare ravioli according to package directions. Drain and lay on paper towels to blot excess water.

In a frying pan melt the butter and sauté garlic until soft. Add the ravioli in batches and fry on each side: 3-4 minutes, or until golden brown. Season with salt and pepper.

Transfer to a decorative plate and garnish with cheese and parsley. Before serving drizzle with a quality olive oil.

The ravioli can
be cooked a day ahead.
Store in a single layer
and keep refrigerated until
ready to fry and serve hot
to your guests.

OLD WORLD OLIVE CO.

To keep the flavors Italian, try Tuscan Herb.
Looking for spicy? Try Tunisian Harissa. Love the taste of
roasted sweet onions? Try Cilantro and Roasted Onion..

Joy's Tips & Tricks

Pot Shiner

DID YOU KNOW?

Olive oil is great for shining your stainless steel pots and pans? You still have to clean them as you always do, but using the oil will add a great shine when you rub a bit on and then buff with a soft cloth.

THE JOY

Before our cooking segments on tv, Joy and I always rub a bit of olive oil, with a cloth, over the outside surfaces of the pans we are using. It makes it easy for us to then wipe off any spills, or last-minute finger prints, just before we go on camera. I find myself doing this at home too, especially when having dinner guests. I don't like it when your beautiful soup, or stew, is sitting on the stove in a big pot with those unsightly sponge swipes. You know what I'm talking about! After you wipe up any spillover, it's a snap to shine-up your pot before any guests see it!

Keep your soft
cloth handy, but hidden,
in a drawer close-by, or the
cabinet nearest the stove.
This way, you can swipe and
get your shine on when no
one is looking!

Judy's Tips & Tricks

Wedding Bell Soup

THE JOY

This is a special dish in the Italian home. Our Great grandmother Nellie always made this soup, and our Nana has passed it on to us. For our family, this delicate soup was always served after the antipasto in Nana's beautiful china soup bowls that she received from her parents as a wedding gift. Truly heartwarming and delicious! Mom insisted that this be served at all of our weddings with a drizzle of olive oil floating gracefully on the top! It looks like a lot for this soup to come together, but it really is easy!

WEDDING BELL SOUP

- 2 cloves garlic, sliced
- 3-4 tablespoons olive oil
- 2 carrots, chopped very small
- 8 cups of chicken broth, (homemade or store bought)
- 2 medium heads of escarole, cleaned and chopped
- S'wepper to taste (salt with pepper), recipe follows*
- 1/4 cup Parmesan cheese
- 2 cups of cooked pasta, anything small, we like pastina

In a 6-quart sauce pan, saute the garlic in olive oil: 2 -3 minutes. Add the chicken broth and bring to a boil for 5 minutes, reduce heat to medium.

Drop the meatballs (recipe follows) into the broth and add the chopped escarole. When the meatballs rise to the top they are just about done, but cook at least 20 minutes more in broth (double check to see if they are cooked through). Add the Parmesan cheese and taste before adding S'wepper (Parmesan cheese is salty) Add the 2 cups cooked macaroni, done! Enjoy!

MINI MEATBALLS

- 1 pound ground beef
- 1/2 cup plain bread crumbs
- 1/4 cup chopped parsley
- 1 egg, lightly beaten
- 1/2 cup grated parmesan cheese
- 1 teapoon S'wepper (salt with pepper), recipe follows*
- 1 clove of garlic, very finely chopped
- 1/4 teaspoon garlic powder (or to taste)
- 1/4 teaspoon onion powder

Mix all the ingredients together and roll into tiny meatballs. I used a well rounded tablespoon to measure these tiny gems!

*S'wepper: a mix of salt & pepper. Two parts salt to one part pepper. Mix, store and ready to go!

OLD WORLD OLIVE CO.

HEALTHY TIPS AND SUBSTITUTIONS

No garlic on hand? Substitute Garlic EVOO

Keep your soft
cloth handy, but hidden,
in a drawer close—by, or the
cabinet nearest the stove.
This way, you can swipe and
get your shine on when no
one is looking!

Joy's Tips & Tricks

Rigatoni

Linguine
al Nero

Farfalle
Tricolore

Pappardelle

Ruote

Pasta Shapes

Eliche
Tricolori

Lumache

Linguine

- Thin, delicate pastas, like angel hair or thin spaghetti, are better served with light, thin sauces.
- Thicker pasta shapes, like fettuccine, work well with heavier sauces.
- Pasta shapes with holes or ridges, like mostaccioli or radiatore, are perfect for chunkier sauces.

Farfalle

Creste di Galli

Linguine
Pomodoro

Penne Tricolori

Tagliolini

Conchiglie

Conchiglioni Verdi
+ Pomorodoro

Chifferini

Fusilli Lunghi

There are almost
as many different pasta
shapes as we have cousins,
don't hesitate trying new
shapes. Just watch those
cooking times. If the pasta
fits...enjoy it!

Judy and Joy say:

· 55 ·

Herbs

BASIL: One of the most popular herbs used in Italian cuisine. It's a necessity for pesto, and it pairs beautifully with tomatoes—the sweetness of the basil balances nicely with the acidity of the tomatoes.

BAY LEAF: Mostly used in soups and stews, make sure to remove the leaves before serving.

MARJORAM: Closely related to Oregano (and can be used as an alternative), however it's flavor is milder and more delicate.

MINT: There are hundreds of varieties of mint. These herbs run the gamut from mild and sweet to spicy and hot. Mint brings a unique freshness to recipes.

OREGANO: Marjoram's wild and more pungent, cousin. An essential ingredient in pizza sauce.

PARSLEY: Many people think of parsley as just a garnish; however, it is widely used in Italian cooking—especially the flat-leaf variety. Note: chewing on fresh parsley will eliminate the smell of garlic from your breath.

ROSEMARY: It's scent has been described as a combination of pine and mint. Rosemary is one of the strongest herbs, so use sparingly, a natural complement to potatoes, chicken, lamb, and beef.

SAGE: Is especially popular in Tuscany. A savory herb, frequently used in butter sauces.

THYME: The small thyme leaves pack a surprising punch; excellent for recipes where an earthy flavor is desired.

Red Sauces

- Spaghetti & Meatballs
- Penne alla Vodka
- Bolognese Sauce
- Lasagna
- Pasta Puttanesca

Spaghetti & Meatballs

THE JUDY

Spaghetti & meatballs is one of my favorite Italian dishes. In our house it was always served on Sunday. One side of the family called it pasta and sauce, while the other side called it macaroni and gravy. Whatever you call it, it's full of white flour and way too many carbohydrates, add to that the calorie-laden meatballs and you have a very heavy meal. I love my healthier, lighter version of this classic that can be eaten anytime—not just for Sunday dinner—even twice a week.

For the sauce (or gravy), I love to use fresh ripe tomatoes. My choice for pasta is usually whole wheat; it's full of fiber with tons of vitamins and nutrients. I also select a very lean beef for the meatballs and mix-in healthier whole wheat bread crumbs rather than white.

Mangia!

JUDY'S HEALTHIER-SHORTER RECIPE

5 pounds of plum tomatoes	1 teaspoon fresh basil, chopped
1/4 cup Old World Olive Co. olive oil (Arbequina or Arbosona recommended)	salt and pepper to taste
4-5 cloves of garlic, chopped	a sprinkling of grated Parmesan cheese
1/4 cup fresh parsley, chopped	

Rinse tomatoes, core and cut in half. Place in a blender, or food processor, and puree until smooth. Set aside.

In a large heated saucepan add the garlic and sauté until golden. Add the tomatoes and remaining ingredients simmer for one hour.

MEATBALLS

1/4 cup of cooked brown rice	3/4 cup grated Parmesan cheese
1/4 cup whole wheat bread crumbs	1/4 cup chopped flat-leaf parsley
2 large eggs, lightly beaten	salt and freshly ground black pepper
3 tablespoons milk	1 pound ground beef (90 percent lean or a ground sirloin)
2 cloves garlic, minced	

Mix all of the ingredients together and shape into balls. Drop meatballs into simmering tomato sauce and let cook for about 45 minutes.

DID YOU KNOW?

The dish spaghetti & meatballs was created to please the American palate, and their preference to have meat served with their pasta. You won't find this in Italy!

Italians call their meatballs polpette, which means, "little meatball". Each family developed their own unique recipe and passed it down from generation to generation.

OLD WORLD OLIVE CO.

HEALTHY TIPS AND SUBSTITUTIONS

Substitute oil and garlic for same proportion of OWOC Garlic olive oil.

Everyone loves fresh herbs, but not everyone has access to an herb garden especially year round. We have the perfect solution: OWOC infused olive oils—the perfect herb garden at your fingertips.
Try: Basil olive oil, Cilantro and roasted garlic olive oil, Sage and Mushroom olive oil, even Garlic olive oil

It's the non-gardener's best friend!

Spaghetti & Meatballs

THE JOY

There is nothing better than the time-honored way to prepare spaghetti & meatballs. I remember Nana and Papa coming to visit from West Hartford to spend weekends with us. Papa was always carrying a big silver pot filled with Nana's heavenly red sauce, chock-full of the best meatballs ever! Every time I serve this family favorite, I giggle to myself at the memory of Papa coming in the front door of our childhood home carrying the Sunday sauce with the 'Italian elbow'!

Bon appetite Papa!

P.S. *'Italian elbow' refers to ringing the doorbell with your bent arm because your hands are busy carrying a pot filled with something delicious!*

TOMATO SAUCE

½	cup Old World Olive Oil (any regional)	1½ - 2	cans of water (use cans from tomatoes)
2	large onions, finely chopped	½	glass red wine (more if you like)
4	cloves garlic, finely chopped		basil, chopped, optional
2	32 ounce cans crushed tomatoes	½	cup Parmesan cheese
1	32 ounce can tomato sauce		salt and black pepper to taste
2	tablespoons tomato paste		garlic and onion powder*

Sauté onions in ½ cup of oil for about 5 minutes, add the garlic and cook 1 minute more. Do not burn the garlic, it will become bitter. Add the 2 cans of crushed tomatoes, 1 can tomato sauce, and 2 tablespoons tomato paste. Let cook about 15 minutes and stir. Add water and stir until sauce comes to a medium boil. Add the wine, grated cheese and basil (if using). Stir then lower heat and allow to a simmer for about 2 hours. Taste and re-season adding garlic and onion powder* and enjoy!

*Mom adds a sprinkle of garlic and onion powder at the end. Stir and continue simmering.

"The tomato paste will help the sauce stick to the pasta". My mother must have said this 10 times to me on the day we were reviewing this recipe...I got it Mom...add the tomato paste!!

JOY'S TRADITIONAL MEATBALLS

½	cup plain bread crumbs	2	garlic cloves, minced
¼	cup flat-leaf parsley, chopped	½	teaspoon salt
2	large eggs, lightly beaten	¾	teaspoon freshly ground black pepper
2	tablespoons whole milk	1½	pound ground beef
¾	cup grated romano or Parmesan cheese		

Mix all the ingredients together and roll into balls any size you like! Drop meatballs into the simmering sauce for at least 1 hour.

Before rolling all of the meatballs, Nana would make a very tiny meatball the size of a quarter and drop it into the sauce, let it cook about 15 minutes then taste it. She did this so she could add more of anything if she needed to!

A great way to get your family accustomed to whole-wheat pasta is to mix whole-wheat and white flour pasta together and ease into it. Soon they won't even notice!

GLUTEN FREE TIP: use cornmeal, hominy grits or gluten free bread to replace traditional breadcrumbs. For the Pasta use your favorite gluten free pasta with ribbons of zucchini. *All Old World Olive Co. products are gluten free.*

Mom always said if the sauce is bitter, add a whole carrot or two and let it cook in the sauce. A pinch of sugar is a favorite trick of Nana's too!

Joy's Tips & Tricks

Penne alla Vodka

THE JUDY

This is a great dish, but ohhhh...so fattening. I have tried over, and over, to make this dish using less butter, a fat-free cream and just a sprinkle of Parmesan cheese. It didn't work. To me, it's just not worth it. I feel, if you are going to eat Penne alla Vodka, then go ahead and enjoy it, just start your diet the next day. However, being forced to make it less hard on the thighs and belly for the sake of this book, I did play around with the recipe. I experimented, changing this, trying that, all to get rid of some of the fat and calories. After days of testing recipes it happened! I came up with a cold penne pasta salad with a bacon vodka dressing. Just remember, this recipe is for adults only.

COLD PENNE PASTA SALAD WITH A BACON VODKA VINAIGRETTE ALLA TINI

- 8 ounces penne pasta, cooked
- 1/2 cup small grape tomatoes
- 1/4 cup shallots
  shaved Parmesan cheese

THE VINAIGRETTE

- 3 tablespoons minced shallots
- 3 tablespoons red wine vinegar
- 3 tablespoons bacon vodka or to taste
- 3 tablespoons Old World Olive Oil

- 2 tablespoons honey
- 1/2 teaspoon salt
- 1/4 teaspoon freshly ground black pepper

DID YOU KNOW?
Vodka adds a unique flavor when cooked with tomatoes. Some people say it adds a peppery flavor or a hint of citrus.

In a bowl, whisk together the shallots, red wine vinegar, bacon vodka, olive oil, honey, salt and black pepper. Toss with cooked pasta and the remaining ingredients.

Try using whole-wheat or gluten free pasta.

Penne alla Vodka

THE JOY

What can I say? This is the ultimate comfort food...fabulous and fattening. And with the edition of the salty bacon, I'm in heaven.

JOY'S PENNE ALLA VODKA RECIPE

- 1 tablespoon Old World Olive Co. oil, once around the pan in a slow stream
- 2 tablespoons butter, or substitute Old World Olive Co. Natural Butter oil
- 3 cloves garlic, minced
- 3 shallots, minced
- 1/2 cup vodka

- 1 cup chicken stock
- 1 32 ounce can crushed tomatoes
  salt and fresh ground pepper
- 16 ounces pasta, such as penne or penne rigatte
- 1/2 cup heavy cream

Heat a large skillet over moderate heat. Add the oil, butter, and shallots. Gently sauté the shallots for three to five minutes to develop their sweetness. Add the garlic and cook for 1 minute. Pour the vodka into pan and reduce by half: 2-3 minutes. Add the chicken stock and tomatoes. Bring sauce to a slow bubble and reduce heat to simmer. Season with salt and pepper.

While the sauce is simmering away, cook your pasta of choice until al dente. Drain.

Stir cream into sauce. When the sauce returns to a small bubble, remove from heat. Toss the hot pasta with sauce.

OLD WORLD OLIVE CO.

HEALTHY TIPS AND SUBSTITUTIONS

There is a healthier option for butter—OWOC Natural Butter Olive Oil. This dairy-free, butter flavored olive oil is the perfect substitute for butter. Here are three prominent benefits of using Natural Butter Olive Oil:

1. It tastes just like butter, but has no dairy. Still 120 calories, but they are mono-saturated calories–healthy fat!
2. Natural Butter Oil is gluten free, vegan and 100% organic.
3. You use a lesser amount. For every 1 cup of butter, substitute only 3/4 cup of butter olive oil. Plus, it has a high smoke point–400 degrees.

So let's hear it for the perfect butter—well, actually, it's better than butter—it's OWOC Natural Butter olive oil.

DID YOU KNOW?

Along with people disco dancing at chic supper clubs in the mid 1970s, the very trendy Penne alla Vodka also came into fashion. And it continues to be one of the most popular dishes today.

My girls are always watching their weight, because of this I have switched from using heavy cream to fat-free half & half. It tastes fabulous and works beautifully in this recipe!

Joy's Tips & Tricks

Bolognese Sauce

THE JUDY

I adore classic Bolognese sauce...it is probably one of my favorites. I really love when Joy makes her sauce with beef, pork, veal and heavy cream—yes I said heavy cream! When it simmers on low for hours at a time, the entire house fills with the comforting aroma of...well, our Nana. Bolognese is a chunky, hearty, heavy sauce, full of calories and fat. And certainly not something you can make and serve in 30 minutes. It needs time, it has to simmer; so I am lightening it up and making it healthier. Plus it will be ready in a snap!

The most dramatic modification I made was to replace the meats with a bean. I love this, and I know you will too. I chose red kidney beans because they are high in fiber, low in fat (a lot lower), and they add a wonderful creaminess to the dish.

RED BEAN BOLOGNESE

- 1 14-ounce can red kidney beans, or other beans, rinsed and drained
- 2 tablespoons Old World Olive Co. olive oil (recommend Coratina or Piqual)
- 1 small onion, chopped
- ½ cup chopped carrot
- ¼ cup chopped celery
  salt to taste
- 4 cloves garlic, chopped
- ½ cup white or red wine (whichever one you prefer)
- 1 14 ounce can diced tomatoes
- ¼ cup chopped fresh parsley, divided
- 8 ounces whole-wheat fettuccine
- ½ cup freshly grated Parmesan cheese

Prepare the whole wheat fettucini according to package directions, set aside.

Heat the oil in a medium saucepan over medium heat. Add the onion, carrot, celery and a sprinkling of salt and cook until softened: 10 minutes. Add the garlic cook 1 minute. Add the wine, increase heat to medium high and boil until most of the liquid evaporates: 3-4 minutes. Add the diced tomatoes, 2 tablespoons parsley and kidney beans. Bring to a low simmer for 15 minutes. Spoon into a food processor and whirl until the mixture is somewhat smooth, more like a sauce.

For a fabulous presentation, I decided to roast a tomato and scoop out the insides. I drizzled the tomato with olive oil and broiled it until the skin blistered. Be careful, you must watch it; or the tomato will burn. Mix the pasta and sauce together before filling.

OLD WORLD OLIVE CO.

HEALTHY TIPS AND SUBSTITUTIONS

Tuscan Herb olive oil is an Italian must for any pasta recipe. It substi-
tutes well for other plain olive oils and is perfect for bread dipping.

Drizzle our 18-Year Traditional balsamic vinegar for
a finishing, crowd-pleasing touch!

Bolognese Sauce

THE JOY

I have a large family; including four daughters with tons of friends, who are always at my house. They like to eat before cheerleading practice and after, before work and after...so pretty much all the time. I love to serve this recipe because once it is cooked; I can just leave it on the stove all day. The kids can then boil up fresh pasta anytime and just top it with the sauce.

DID YOU KNOW?

Bolognese Sauce is a tomato based meat sauce that is simmered with carrots, onions and celery.

The recipe originated in Bologna, Italy, and is called a ragu. There are little or no tomatoes in the recipe. In 1982 a recipe was registered with the Academia Italiana Della Cucina, which is supposedly the most authentic.

JOY'S TRADITIONAL RECIPE

1/4	pound pancetta, diced
1	medium size onion, diced
1	medium carrot, peeled diced
1	medium rib celery, diced
4	garlic cloves, minced
2	tablespoons Old World Olive Co. Olive Oil (Recommend: Coratina or Piqual)
1/2	pound ground sirloin
1/2	pound ground veal

1/2	pound ground pork
1/2 to 1	teaspoon sea salt (I like fine sea salt, but any is fine)
1/4	teaspoon freshly ground black pepper
1	32 ounce can crushed tomatoes
1/2	glass dry red wine
1/2	cup milk or cream (I use fat-free half & half and it works fine)
	grated cheese for sprinkling

Heat the olive oil in large sauce pot. Cook the pancetta and minced vegetables on low heat, uncovered for about 30 minutes. Give it a stir every now and then. Add the ground meats, salt, pepper, and brown them up. Add the can of tomatoes and wine and simmer uncovered for about 45 minutes. Add the milk, or cream, a little at a time and stir.

Take a sip of wine, the kids will be home from school soon...with all of their friends.

Instead of chopping the celery, carrots and onions, a quick whirl in the food processor has the job done in seconds!

Lasagna

THE JUDY

Lasagna soup was a huge hit with my family, the only complaint was that there wasn't enough for leftovers. I broke the lasagna noodles into big chunks. They have a perfect chewy texture (al dente of course), and swimming in a rich tomato broth; it was sheer bliss. I topped the soup with a scoop of creamy Parmesan ricotta in the center—it took my breath away. So simple, and so fast to make; who the heck wants to make it the traditional way? NOT ME!

LASAGNA SOUP

2 -3	tablespoons Old World Olive Co. olive oil (Recommend Koronneicki or Nocellara)
1	pound ground Italian sausage
1	onion, diced
2	cloves garlic, chopped
2	pounds fresh tomatoes (I used campari tomatoes)
2	tablespoons tomato paste

4	cups chicken broth (I used store bought)
	salt and pepper to taste
¼-½	cups grated Parmesan cheese
½	cup red wine
½	pound lasagna noodles broken into large pieces

Heat the oil in a large soup pot. Add the sausage and cook until browned. Add the onions and garlic cook for another 3-4 minutes. Add the tomatoes, chicken broth, tomato paste, wine and Parmesan cheese. Let simmer for an hour, taste and re-season.

About 10 minutes before you are ready to serve add the torn lasagna noodles to the soup pot. They may take a bit longer to cook, so keep checking. More broth may need to be added at this point to compensate for the large chunks of noodles. I also brought another pot of salted water to a boil in order to cook some additional noodles.

Ladle the soup into big bowls and top with a dollop of ricotta right in the center! Crusty bread is the perfect accompaniment.

Any shape pasta will work perfectly in this dish.

PARMESAN RICOTTA

4	ounces ricotta
¼	cup Parmesan, grated
¼	mozzarella, shredded

1	tablespoon basil and parsley, chopped
	salt and pepper to taste

Mix all the ingredients together (except for the salt and pepper), check for saltiness before adding any salt, the Parmesan cheese is salty on its own. Season with pepper

GLUTEN FREE SUGGESTION

Gluten free lasagna noodles and brown rice noodles are available; if not in your supermarket, try a speciality food store. An even healthier choice would be to replace the noodles with slices of zucchini or eggplant, or try a combination of both!

DID YOU KNOW?

The time consuming task of boiling noodles used to be a requirement for lasagna but now no-boil noodles exist!

Lasagna can be made in the dishwasher, are you serious? Yes!!! Prepare your lasagna as normal using whichever noodle you choose (boil or no boil) and cover tightly with aluminum foil. Use the heated dry and sanitize cycle on your dishwasher to cook the lasagna.

The soup is even
better the next day,
a bit thicker and richer
in flavor. So go ahead
and prepare
a day ahead.

Judy's Tips & Tricks

OLD WORLD OLIVE CO.

When serving, drizzle one of our high polyphenol extra
virgin olive oils over the top of the soup as a finishing touch.
This not only adds a burst of flavor, but also provides
a healthy way to get your daily antioxidants! Win/Win!!

All Old World Olive Co. oils and vinegars are gluten free.

Lasagna

THE JOY

Today there are so many different ways to prepare lasagna. It can be made using your favorite meat such as: beef, turkey, chicken, pork, 'saus-a-veech' (that's how we say sausage!), it can even be vegetarian, using fresh vegetables along with a variety cheeses. The sky is the limit when it comes to this amazing dish, so be creative and have fun!

TRADITIONAL LASAGNA RECIPE

Your family sauce recipe
(mine has ground sausage this time)

3   pounds fresh ricotta cheese

3   large egg yolks

1   cup grated Parmesan cheese

Salt to taste

1/4   teaspoon fresh ground black pepper

handful of chopped parsley

1   pound no cook lasagna noodles,
or regular boiled noodles if you prefer

1   pound fresh shredded mozzarella
cheese

Preheat oven to 400 degrees and butter an 11 x 14 x 3-inch baking pan.

Bring sauce to room temperature.

In a large bowl, mix together the ricotta cheese, egg yolks and Parmesan cheese. Stop and taste before you add any salt. Add black pepper and parsley.

Spread about 3 cups of the sauce on the bottom of the prepared baking dish. Place a layer of noodles on top of the sauce, overlap a bit if you wish. Spread about 2 cups of the sauce over the noodles and half of the ricotta mixture on top of the sauce. Top with another layer of lasagna noodles.

Repeat with more sauce and the remaining ricotta mixture. Top with a final layer of lasagna noodles and finish with a layer of shredded mozzarella.

Bake until the sauce is bubbling and the cheese is melted, at least 1 hour. If the cheese starts to brown, cover with aluminum foil. Let the lasagna stand 10-15 minutes before serving.

Sauce can be prepared a day ahead of time.

DID YOU KNOW?
Originally, the word "lasagna" did not refer to the food, instead "lasagna" denoted the dish it was cooked in. The earliest lasagna recipes date back to the thirteenth century. Europeans were not familiar with tomatoes at that time, and so tomatoes were not even used in initial versions of lasagna.

OLD WORLD OLIVE CO.

A fun twist on this fan favorite is to drizzle Old World Olive Co. Porcini olive oil over the top – it gives the dish an earthy, flavorful bite.

Cover unbaked, and refrigerate up to one day in advance, or freeze, unbaked, up to three weeks in advance. Defrost overnight in the refrigerator; bake as directed.

Joy's Tips & Tricks

To check if the lasagna is hot through out, Mom would stick a butter knife carefully into the middle and hold it there for a few seconds. If the knife is hot to the touch when you pull it out, it is ready to go!

Pasta Puttanesca

THE JUDY

Chickpeas (garbanzo beans) are a perfect match for this thick Italian red sauce. Actually, I prefer my puttanesca with chickpeas, rather than on pasta, and I feel better after eating it. It's a wonderful alternative if you are sensitive to gluten.

JUDY'S PUTTANESCA WITH CHICK PEAS

1 pound fresh tomatoes, diced	1/4 cup parsley, finely chopped
8 anchovy fillets, minced	3-4 cloves garlic, minced or pressed
1/2 cup pitted Kalamata olives, coarsely chopped	2-3 tablespoons Old World olive oil
3 tablespoons capers, rinsed	1 teaspoon red chili flakes
	2 cups canned chickpeas

Press or finely mince the garlic. Heat a large pan on medium and add 2 tablespoons olive oil. When the olive oil swirls easily in the pan add the anchovies, garlic mixture and chili flakes. Stir continuously until garlic just begins to brown, about 2 minutes, add the tomatoes and simmer.

Allow tomatoes to cook, stirring occasionally. If the tomatoes begin to stick to the bottom of the pan, add 1/4 cup water to thin the sauce. You may need to do this several times depending upon the variety of tomato. When the tomatoes begin to soften, use a wooden spoon to crush them a bit in the pan to create smaller chunks.

After the sauce has simmered about 12-15 minutes toss in the capers, olives, and parsley. Mix to combine. I toss in some excellent olive oil at this point to brighten it up.

Pepper is a nice addition, but salt is probably not necessary because of the anchovies.

To save time, use a chopped tomato in the box.

Pasta Puttanesca

DID YOU KNOW?

There are three very funny Italian tales about this hot and spicy sauce.

1. Bordello ladies preferred this easy sauce because it could be made quickly between servicing customers.

2. Wives would throw leftovers of the pasta dish while screaming, Puttana, Puttana! at the above mentioned ladies as they walked by.

3. The sauce was a favorite of married women who wanted to spend less time in the kitchen; and more time with their husbands in the bedroom!

THE JOY

The traditional pasta paired with this recipe is spaghetti, but any pasta your family prefers is just fine! We have used all types: penne, buccatini (Judy's favorite) and linguini. The dish is tangy and a bit salty from the capers; as for spice, you can make it as hot as you like. When we were teens, every time our mom served this dish for dinner, she would tell us a silly story that long ago the ladies of the evening would place pots of puttanesca in their windows to tempt men into their bordellos. We would laugh trying to picture this story in our minds as we shoveled forkfuls of the delicious spaghetti into our mouths.

JOYS TRADITIONAL RECIPE

¼ cup Old World Olive Oil	2 tablespoons drained capers
1 cup finely chopped onion	2 tablespoons minced anchovy fillets (about 8 fillets)
6 cloves minced garlic	½ teaspoon dried crushed basil
2 28 ounce cans Roma plum tomatoes, crushed with juice	½ teaspoon dried crushed red pepper flakes
1 cup tightly packed, pitted, and halved Kalamata olives	Salt, optional (taste first)
2 tablespoons tomato paste	1 pound penne pasta, cooked al dente

In a large pot heat the olive oil over medium high heat. Add the onion and sauté until soft and lightly caramelized, about 6 minutes. Add the garlic and cook an additional 2 minutes. Add the tomatoes and the remaining ingredients and simmer until the sauce has thickened and is slightly reduced: 40 minutes. Adjust seasoning to taste, cover and set aside. Add the spaghetti to the pan and stir.

Cream Sauces

- Fettuccini Alfredo
- Lemon Creme Sauce
- Spaghetti Carbonara
- Tiramisu

Fettuccine Alfredo

THE JUDY

Thank God there is a lighter, healthier approach for this fabulous dish! The yogurt blended with the ricotta cheese makes a wonderful, light sauce; mild in flavor, completely satisfying, and totally guilt free! I like to use Greek yogurt rather than regular because it has a thicker, creamier texture and is higher in protein than most other yogurts. I am so happy about this dish; I love to lighten up my recipes for my body, and this one feeds my soul too!

JUDY'S HEALTHY VERSION FETTUCCINE ALFREDO

- 8 ounces angel hair pasta
- 1 tablespoon or more of Old World olive oil, or try Old World Olive Co. Natural Butter Olive Oil
- 1 shallot, sliced
- 1 garlic clove minced
  (some times I sprinkle on garlic powder instead, 1/4 teaspoon)
- 1 cup low-fat plain Greek yogurt

- 1 cup low-fat ricotta cheese
- 1/2 cup Parmesan cheese
- 1/2 teaspoon lemon zest, optional
  kosher salt to taste, check sauce first before adding
  freshly ground black pepper
  reserved pasta water

Boil and cook the pasta according to package directions. Drain well, reserving about 1 cup of the pasta water.

In a large skillet on medium high heat add the olive oil and sauté shallots until soft. Add the garlic and cook a few minutes longer. Lower the heat to medium low and add the yogurt, low-fat ricotta, Parmesan cheese and lemon zest (if you are using it). Stir with a wooden spoon. If the sauce is too thick, add the pasta water one spoonful at a time.* Continue to stir and add more water until desired consistency is reached. Add the pasta to sauce pan and toss to coat, serve immediately.

This is a great technique to thin the sauce to your preferred texture.

 For a quick protein boost add shrimp or chicken.

Replace the pasta entirely by using ribbons of zucchini squash to cut even more carbs and calories.

Judy's Tips & Tricks

OLD WORLD OLIVE CO.

HEALTHY TIPS AND SUBSTITUTIONS

Too add a boost of lemon flavor, try using our Milanese Gremalata olive oil, it pairs our quality olive oil with the zest of fresh lemons. A great option for when you don't have any lemons in the house.

For even more lemony goodness, may we suggest Old World Olive Co. Sicilian Lemon balsamic vinegar for a burst of lemon. Don't be afraid to experiment, this vinegar has only 10 calories per tablespoon. It tastes great and balsamics aid in digestion.

Fettuccine Alfredo

THE JOY

There is something about a bowl of creamy Fettuccine Alfredo that makes my mouth water. In this recipe the cream, butter, cheeses, and subtle flavor of garlic make a delightful sauce that perfectly coats the pasta. I love the way the pasta slips through my lips surrounded by the velvety sauce. Yum! This isn't a light dish, and certainly not the healthiest, but you need to spoil yourself every now and then. Judy likes to remind me that every once in a while a little indulgence is good for your spirit.

FETTUCCINE ALFREDO

1 pound fettuccine noodles cooked and drained, reserve some of the pasta water

1 stick butter or substitute with 6 tablespoons Old World Olive Co. Natural Butter olive oil

3 garlic cloves, sliced

1 cup heavy cream
salt and pepper, to taste

1½ cups freshly grated Parmesan cheese, start with this you can add more if you like

Cook pasta according to package directions.

In a warm saucepan or skillet, melt the butter, add garlic and cook one minute. Add the cream and season with freshly ground black pepper. Sprinkle in half of the cheese and stir, check for saltiness before sprinkling on the salt. Add pasta, toss.

At this point you may need to add some of the reserved pasta water to thin the sauce. Add in the rest of the Parmesan cheese, toss quickly and serve immediately.

Gluten Free or brown rice pasta can be substituted

DID YOU KNOW?

Fettuccine Alfredo bears the name of its creator, Alfredo di Lelio who operated a restaurant in Rome. Legend has it; he improvised a basic pasta dish with butter and cheese so that his pregnant wife (who was suffering from morning sickness) would find it appealing enough to eat. Apparently the recipe worked. He then served it in his restaurant where it became a big hit... and it remains a big hit on both sides of the Atlantic!

OLD WORLD OLIVE CO.

Fettuccini Alfredo is absolutely divine with
a tablespoon or two of our White Truffle oil
stirred into the sauce just before serving,
or added individually to each plate.

A great way
to thin the sauce
is by adding a little
of the hot pasta
water to it.

Joy's Tips & Tricks

Lemon Cream Sauce

I love the freshness that lemons bring to any recipe. Our mom would say, "It just brightens it up a bit". And she is right. I often find myself saying, "What does this recipe need?" And the answer usually is "it needs a bit of citrus". While I was working on this healthier recipe for lemon cream sauce, I knew fresh lemon zest would help balance the twang of the yogurt. The result is a bright, fresh sauce.

PASTA WITH LEMON CREAM SAUCE

- 8 ounces pasta, whole wheat, gluten free or high-protein pasta
- 1/2 cup nonfat Greek yogurt
- 1/4 cup grated Parmesan cheese
- 1-2 teaspoon(s) grated lemon zest
- 1/4 teaspoon salt, taste first

- 1/4 teaspoon cracked black pepper
- 1-2 tablespoon(s) olive oil
- 2 garlic cloves, minced
- 1/2 shallot, minced
- 2 tablespoons parsley, minced
- 2 tablespoons chives, minced

Boil pasta according to package directions and set aside, I used cavatappi for this presentation. Save 1/4 cup pasta water.

In a skillet on medium heat, sauté shallots and garlic in olive oil until soft: 3-4 minutes. Add the yogurt, Parmesan, salt, pepper and lemon zest.

Add in the drained pasta. Stir to combine and add some of the reserved pasta water and taste it. Adjust any seasoning to your liking. A sprinkling of parsley and chives for the garnish, and you're good to go!

OLD WORLD OLIVE CO.

HEALTHY TIPS AND SUBSTITUTIONS

Who would resist a swapping butter for oil when it means
less fat (and a healthier fat), lower calories while keeping the same
great taste! OWOC Natural Butter olive oil is at your service. May we
also suggest adding OWOC Meyer Lemon olive oil for an
authentic Italian lemon flavor.

Lemon Cream Sauce

THE JOY

This is a great spring dish, and a favorite of ours at Easter time. A few years ago when I was in Italy we had this dish at a local restaurant. The lemons were as big as oranges and much sweeter than we have here in the states. The lemon flavor adds a hint of brightness and makes the sauce so refreshing.

SPAGHETTI WITH LEMON CREAM SAUCE AND ASPARAGUS

1 pound asparagus	3 tablespoons butter or substitute
2 large shallots	2 tablespoons Old World Olive Co.
2 lemons	Natural Butter Olive Oil
1 pound dried spaghetti or fettuccine	$^3/_4$ cup heavy cream

Trim the asparagus, cut on diagonal into $^1/_4$-inch thick slices. Finely chop the shallots. Finely grate lemon zest to measure $1^1/_2$ teaspoons, and squeeze enough juice to measure 3 tablespoons.

Cook the asparagus in boiling water until tender and yet still crisp, about 3 minutes. Drain and set aside.

In a deep 12-inch heavy skillet cook the shallots in butter on low heat: 5 minutes. Season with salt and pepper to taste. Stir in the cream and zest. Simmer, then add 2 tablespoons lemon juice. Take skillet off the heat.

Cook the pasta in boiling water until al dente in firmness. Reserve 1 cup pasta water. Drain pasta and add to sauce along with the asparagus, $^1/_2$ cup pasta water, remaining tablespoon lemon juice, and salt and pepper to taste. Heat mixture over low heat and toss.

DID YOU KNOW?

Lemon Cream Sauce is extremely versatile. As a savory sauce, it's great when flavored with garlic, basil and Parmesan cheese served over pasta, chicken, veal or fish. But it's also a wonderful dessert sauce and can be used in cupcakes, puddings, as a cake filling, or even just on its own.

OLD WORLD OLIVE CO.

We bring zing! A splash of Old World Olive Co. Sicilian Lemon
Balsamic Vinegar adds a subtle, yet bright bit of flavor.
Or simply drizzle Old World Olive Co. Meyer
Lemon olive oil as a finishing touch.

A fresh grating
of lemon zest on top
adds extra zing and looks
fabulous. You can also
decorate the plate with a
lemon slice or an edible
pansy...perfect for
a spring meal!

Joy's Tips & Tricks

Pasta Carbonara

THE JUDY

I love this recipe but don't understand why it couldn't be just as fabulous with healthier ingredients. All that fat from the cream and the bacon is a heart attack waiting to happen, and just not necessary. I always substitute heavy cream with a fat-free half & half or fat-free cream for my cream based sauces...my family never knows the difference! Replacing regular bacon with turkey bacon is a beneficial choice as well. It's delicious and has 50% less fat than regular bacon..

JUDY'S HEALTHY SPAGHETTI CARBONARA

- 8 ounces brown rice pasta
- 1 cup Egg Beaters®
- ½ cup shredded Parmesan cheese
  splash of fat free heavy cream (optional, I love a splash or two of this)
- 1 tablespoon Old World Olive Co. olive oil
- 3 shallots, chopped

- 3 cloves garlic, minced
- ½ cup parsley, chopped, saving some for garnish
- 1 teaspoon ground black pepper
  salt to taste
- 2 slices of turkey bacon cooked for crumbling on top, (½ slice of bacon for each, more if you want)

Cook pasta in a large pot.

In a large skillet add the olive oil and sauté shallots until soft. Add the garlic and cook one more minute. Turn heat down to low.

In a separate bowl beat the Egg Beaters®, Parmesan cheese, parsley (about half) and cream (if using) add to skillet and stir until combined.

Drain the pasta and add to skillet. Toss quickly until egg mixture cooks.

Sprinkle with the turkey bacon crumbles.

The splash of fat-free cream adds creaminess to the dish with out all the calories. You can also use fat-free evaporated milk.

Use any pasta
you like. Whole wheat
or spinach would be delish.
I like brown rice pasta
a lot, it's light, and doesn't
cause bloating the
way regular
pasta does.

Judy's Tips & Tricks

Pasta Carbonara

THE JOY

This recipe is truly my favorite. I know that I say that about all of my recipes, but this one is de-lush. There is just no other word. The eggy sauce clings to each strand of the spaghetti perfectly, and with a very generous helping of grated Parmesan cheese and heavy cream...this recipe goes right to ah-maz-ing!

PASTA CARBONARA

- 1 pound pasta, cooked al dente (any kind)
- 5 eggs
- ½ cup heavy cream

  salt and freshly ground black pepper to taste
- 1 tablespoon Old World Olive Co. olive oil

- 2 tablespoons butter or substitute with Old World Olive Co. Natural Butter olive oil
- ½ pound pancetta, bacon, prosciutto or salt pork,
- 3 garlic cloves
- 1¼ cups freshly grated Parmesan and/or romano cheese

Cut the pancetta, bacon, prosciutto or salt pork into small ⅛-inch cubes. Add the 3 whole, peeled garlic cloves.

In a large heavy skillet over low heat, sauté the meat bits and garlic for 10 minutes or so, until the meat becomes translucent and softened. Press the softened garlic into the oil from the bacon. Add additional olive oil as needed to keep bits from sticking.

Meanwhile, cook the pasta until al dente and drain

Beat the eggs and cream together. Add a pinch of salt.

Add butter to pan and stir until melted. Stir the cooked pasta into the skillet. Remove pan from heat and stir in the beaten egg/cream mixture along with half of the grated cheese. Stir quickly as the heat of the pasta will begin to cook the eggs. Stir until each strand of spaghetti is well coated. Toss in remaining cheese. Salt and pepper to taste. Serve at once.

DID YOU KNOW?

This Pasta dish originated in Rome and is said to be the favorite dish of the coal miners. Long ago the men would go out to the woods for months at a time. They packed most of the ingredients for this recipe and would look for fresh eggs at local farms they happened to come upon. The men would cook over an open flame in big cast iron pots, it was a quick and an easy meal for them to toss together at the end of a long day.

OLD WORLD OLIVE CO.

For additional Italian flavor, add Old World Olive Co.
Basil olive oil - perfect fresh basil flavor every time.

Serve a poached
egg on top of each
dish. This puts the presentation way over the top!
You can use a raw egg on
top if it is pasteurized
and you feel safe
doing so.

Joy's Tips & Tricks

IT'S A TRADITION

No matter
where we are,
our meals always
end on a sweet
note.

Tiramisu

THE JUDY

A fabulous dessert and a staple in our home, but packed with way too many calories! After a little thought and experimenting I came up with a lighter version that is still rich in flavor and completely satisfying. Our Aunt Lena used to make a meringue cookie, which we call "schoomie's". Please do not ask us why she chose this silly name—to this day no one knows! They were a crisp meringue flecked with sweet chocolate (always a favorite in our family). I decided to pipe the meringue into kiss shaped cookies and sandwich them with a more healthful filling rather than the traditional mascarpone. The result was bellisimo! Ciao!

COFFEE MERINGUES

4	egg whites (room temperature)		1	cup superfine sugar
¼	teaspoon cream of tartar		2½	teaspoons espresso powder

Preheat oven to 225°F.

Separate the eggs and bring to room temperature (save yolks for another use).

Mix the espresso powder with the superfine sugar.

Place room temperature egg whites in a metal or glass bowl. Begin beating the eggs until they start to thicken. Add the cream of tartar and continue beating eggs until soft peaks form.

Gradually begin to add the sugar to the egg whites. Do this SLOWLY and in a steady stream (while still beating). Continue beating the mixture until it is glossy and stiff peaks form (you'll need to beat the mixture on a high speed at this point). Unsure that the sugar is fully incorporated by running some of the meringue between two fingers, you should not feel any sugar grains.

Line your baking sheet with parchment paper. Spoon the meringue mixture into a piping bag with a large star tip (or like I do, spoon it into a plastic bag and snip the tip off).

Bake for two hours. DO NOT open the door during the baking process. Turn off the oven and let them stay inside the oven until the oven completely cools down.

RICOTTA CHEESE FILLING RECIPE

1	cup part skim ricotta cheese		1	teaspoon rum
2	tablespoons powdered sugar			mini chocolate chips or shavings can be added (optional)
2	teaspoons vanilla extract			

In a small bowl combine the ricotta cheese, powdered sugar, vanilla and rum. Stir thoroughly to combine all of the ingredients, cover and cool in the refrigerator.

ASSEMBLY

Put these together just before serving because the moisture will melt the meringue. Coat one of the meringue kisses on the flat side with ricotta cheese filling and sandwich with another meringue kiss.

In our family,
the meal isn't over
until we've had our
"coffee an…"

Tiramisu

THE JOY

This is the most popular dessert for Italians. While many variations and presentations have evolved over the years, the one consistent ingredient has always been the mascarpone cheese. Traditional Tiramisu made in Italy contained raw eggs; today, because of the danger of salmonella contamination, we prefer to cook the yolks with the sugar in a double boiler to reduce any risk.

JOY'S TRADITIONAL TIRAMISU

6	egg yolks
3	tablespoons sugar
1	pound mascarpone cheese
1½	cups strong espresso, cooled

2	teaspoons dark rum
24	packaged ladyfingers
½	cup bittersweet chocolate shavings, for garnish

Combine the egg yolks and sugar in the top of a double boiler. Beat at medium speed with an electric mixer until thick and lemon-colored. Place over boiling water and reduce heat to medium-low, cook 10 minutes constantly stirring. Add the mascarpone cheese and beat until smooth. Add 1 tablespoon of espresso, mix thoroughly. In a small shallow dish add the remaining espresso and rum.

Dip each ladyfinger into the espresso and rum mixture for 5 seconds. If you let the ladyfingers soak too long, they will fall apart. Place the soaked ladyfingers on the bottom of a 13 x 9-inch baking dish, breaking them in half in order to entirely cover the bottom. Spread ½ of the mascarpone filling over the ladyfingers. Add another layer of soaked ladyfingers and top with remaining mascarpone mix.

Cover tiramisu with plastic wrap and refrigerate for at least 2 hours and up to 8 hours. Before serving sprinkle with chocolate shavings.

 Prepare some extra coffee just in case the quantity is not enough.

DID YOU KNOW?

The name tiramisu means "pick me up" in Italian, because most recipes use ladyfingers soaked in strong espresso coffee along with cocoa powder and mascarpone cheese.

The folk tale surrounding this dessert's popularity is that patrons of Italian bordellos enjoyed the energy boost espresso gave them after their visit. Enterprising madams then concocted tiramisu and served their patrons a healthy portion. They could then go about the rest of their daily activity revitalized, instead of wanting to take a nap.

OLD WORLD OLIVE CO.

Oh but we have a sweet tooth too! Old World Olive Co.
Espresso and Old World Olive Co. Dark Chocolate
Balsamic Vinegar gives the surprising burst of restrained flavor to tiramisu.
These can easily substitute in for the added calories of chocolate sauce,
or the full flavor or espresso.

Balsamic Vinegars help regulate blood sugars,
so this makes dessert for diabetics a little more doable.

We also suggest a drizzle of our Raspberry Balsamic Vinegar
as a fun and unexpected surprise to this dish!

Any coffee
flavored liqueur can
be used; Kahlua®, Brandy
or our special favorite—
Patrón® Tequila XO Café.
Meringues tend to get
soft in humidity,
so eat em' up!

Joy's Tips & Tricks